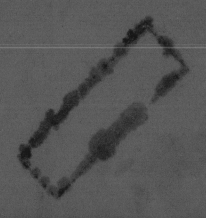

POPULAR
CHINESE COOKERY

Printed by Toppan Printing Co. (S) Pte. Ltd.

FOREWORD

Chinese cuisine, as part of an ancient culture, boasts of a tradition very much its own. Spanning over thousands of years of development, the exquisite flavours hail from the various regions of the country. Recipes from Peking, Szechuan, Canton and Hunan, to name just a few regions, differ in their distinct character and flavour.

Collected within the pages of this book are traditional Chinese dishes originating from kitchens in Hongkong, Taipei and Singapore. The local touch makes these recipes specialities of these countries.

Each recipe in the book is clearly illustrated and explained. Furthermore, all the ingredients are easily obtainable and should not prevent any cook, beginner or expert, to savour some of the best in Chinese cuisine.

CONTENTS

MINCED BEEF WRAPPED IN CABBAGE

INGREDIENTS

500 g minced beef
8 large cabbage leaves, boiled in
water and a little oil until limp
2 slices ginger
2 tablespoons cooking oil

A 1 teaspoon cooking wine
½ teaspoon salt
½ tablespoon oyster sauce
½ tablespoon cornflour
½ tablespoon black soy sauce
1 teaspoon sugar

B 1 tablespoon black soy sauce
5 tablespoons water
1 teaspoon salt
1 tablespoon oyster sauce
1 teaspoon sesame oil
1 teaspoon sugar
1 teaspoon Ve-Tsin

C ½ teaspoon cornflour
1½ tablespoons water

METHOD

1 Marinate minced beef in **A** for ½ hour.
2 Heat 2 tablespoons of cooking oil, fry the 2 slices of ginger then add the minced beef. Remove from heat when beef changes colour.
3 Divide beef into 8 portions and wrap each one in a cabbage leaf. Place in a heat-proof dish and steam for 15 minutes.
4 Bring **B** to the boil and add well-stirred **C**. Cook till slightly thickened.
5 Pour the mixture over the cabbage-wrapped minced beef and serve immediately.

BAKED HAM IN HONEY SAUCE

FRIED CRAB CLAWS

INGREDIENTS

8 crab claws with shells removed
100 g fat pork, minced
100 g lean pork, minced
200 g prawn meat, minced
70 g bamboo shoots, chopped fine
Cornflour for dusting
2 cups cooking oil

A 2 tablespoons cornflour
   2 egg whites
   1 tablespoon chopped spring
   onion
   1 teaspoon salt
   Pinch of Ve-Tsin and pepper

METHOD

1 Combine the minced fat pork, lean
   pork, prawn meat and bamboo
   shoots with **A**.
2 Beat the mixture with a spoon for
   10 minutes and divide into 8
   portions. Coat the crab claws with
   the mixture.
3 Dust the coated crab claws with
   cornflour and deep-fry in oil until a
   golden colour.

BAKED HAM IN HONEY SAUCE

INGREDIENTS

500 g cooked ham
200 g lotus seeds, prepared as on
page 95

A 1 tablespoon honey
   5 tablespoons water
   3 tablespoons tomato sauce

B ½ tablespoon cornflour
   1½ tablespoons water

METHOD

1 Boil lotus seeds in water till cooked.
2 Place lotus seeds with cooked ham
   in a dish. Add 1 tablespoon of
   honey and steam for ½ hour.
   When cooked, pour away excess
   liquid.
3 Bring **A** to the boil. Stir in **B** and
   cook until the mixture slightly
   thickens.
4 Pour the gravy over the ham and
   serve immediately.

SHARK'S FIN SOUP

INGREDIENTS

300 g cleaned and stewed shark's fins
100 g crab meat
1 egg, beaten
5 tablespoons cooking oil

A 4 rice bowls chicken stock
   ½ teaspoon cooking wine
   4 teaspoons salt
   2 teaspoons Ve-Tsin
   2 teaspoons sugar
   ½ tablespoon light soy sauce
   ½ teaspoon sesame oil
   Pinch of pepper

B 5 tablespoons cornflour
   5 tablespoons water

METHOD

1 Heat 5 tablespoons of cooking oil, then add **A** and shark's fins.
2 When mixture slightly boils, add stirred **B** gradually.
3 Add the crab meat and beaten egg, stir again and allow the mixture to boil. Serve hot.

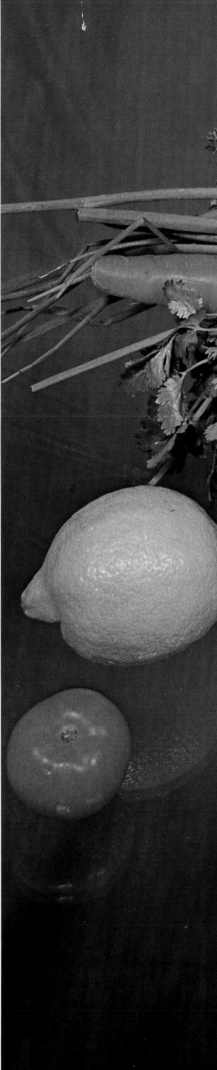

PRAWNS WITH GREEN PEAS

INGREDIENTS

300 g small prawns
50 g roasted cashew nuts
50 g frozen or canned peas
2 slices ginger
3 tablespoons cooking oil

A ½ egg white
   ½ teaspoon salt
   1 tablespoon cornflour

B ½ teaspoon salt
   ½ teaspoon Ve-Tsin
   1 teaspoon cooking wine
   1 teaspoon sesame oil

METHOD

1 Shell and clean prawns. Marinate with **A** for ½ hour.
2 Heat the cooking oil and fry the ginger slices. Add the prawns, then the peas. Stir-fry for a few minutes and add **B**.
3 Remove from heat when prawns are cooked and mix in the roasted cashew nuts. Serve immediately.

ROAST LAMB

INGREDIENTS

1 kg lamb, cut from rolled shoulder of loin chops
4 tablespoons cooking oil

A 4 tablespoons soy sauce
   2 tablespoons cooking wine
   2 cloves garlic, crushed
   1 tablespoon sesame oil
   1 teaspoon ginger, chopped
   1 tablespoon sugar
   juice of ½ lemon

METHOD

1 Slice the lamb into 2 cm slices and marinate in **A** for 1 hour.
2 Preheat oven to 200°C.
3 Pour the cooking oil over the lamb slices and place in oven and roast for 15 minutes.
4 Turn the lamb slices and continue to roast for a further 15 minutes. The total roasting time is 30 minutes.

This recipe is also suitable for a barbecue, using a charcoal fire.

ROAST LEAN PORK

INGREDIENTS

500 g lean pork with some fat, cut
into strips of 6 cm width

A 1 teaspoon Ve-Tsin
   2 teaspoons salt
   4 tablespoons sugar
   1 tablespoon black soy sauce
   1 or 2 drops cochineal
   3 tablespoons water

METHOD

1 Marinate the pork strips in **A** for 4
   to 5 hours.
2 Preheat oven to 220°C. Place pork
   strips on a cooking rack and roast
   for 20 minutes.
3 Remove from oven and baste with
   remaining marinade. Lower oven
   temperature to 190°C and continue
   roasting for another 15 minutes.
4 Remove from oven, cool and slice
   to serve.

BRAISED MUTTON IN SOY SAUCE

INGREDIENTS

500 g mutton, cubed
1 carrot, cubed
1 large onion, cubed
3 slices ginger
3 cloves garlic, chopped
2 tablespoons cooking oil

A 1 tablespoon cooking wine
   1 star anise
   1 stick of cinnamon
   2 tablespoons black soy sauce
   ½ tablespoon light soy sauce
   ½ tablespoon sugar

METHOD

1 Boil mutton cubes in salted water
   for ½ hour. Remove mutton from
   stock.
2 Heat the cooking oil and fry garlic
   and ginger. Add the mutton and
   brown for a few minutes.
3 Add 1 cup of the mutton stock,
   carrot, onion and **A**. Bring to the
   boil and reduce heat to simmer until
   the mutton is tender. Serve hot.

17

BRAISED MUTTON IN SOY SAUCE

PAPER WRAPPED CHICKEN

INGREDIENTS

1 chicken about 1½ kg, cut into
20 pieces
2 tablespoons ginger, shredded
6 stalks spring onions, shredded
100 g cooked ham, shredded
20 sheets greaseproof paper
Oil for deep-frying

A 2 teaspoons salt
   1 teaspoon Ve-Tsin
   1 tablespoon oyster sauce
   ½ tablespoon ginger juice
   2 tablespoons water
   ½ tablespoon cornflour
   1 tablespoon cooking wine
   1 tablespoon cooking oil

METHOD

1 Marinate chicken in **A** for 1 hour.
2 Place each piece of chicken with
ginger, spring onions and ham on
the greaseproof paper. Fold into
envelopes and secure with wire
staples. Fry in hot oil for 8
minutes.
3 Remove and drain. Serve in the
paper envelopes.

LUXURY FRIED EGGS

INGREDIENTS

5 eggs
40 g cooked ham, shredded
1 onion, sliced
40 g roast pork, shredded
2 dried mushrooms, soaked and
shredded
2 tablespoons green peas
1 stalk spring onion, chopped
4 tablespoons cooking oil
A ½ teaspoon salt
½ teaspoon soy sauce
½ teaspoon sesame oil
pinch of pepper
2 tablespoons water

METHOD

1 Beat eggs in a bowl. Add onion
  slices, spring onion, green peas,
  shredded mushrooms, roast pork
  and cooked ham. Add **A** and mix
  well.
2 Heat the cooking oil and fry egg
  mixture until cooked. Garnish with
  a sprig of Chinese parsley.

DUCK SOUP WITH SALTED VEGETABLES

INGREDIENTS

1 medium duck about 1½ kg
300 g salted vegetables, soaked in
water for 1 hour
6 cups water
4 tomatoes
1 preserved sweet lemon
4 cloves garlic, crushed
3 slices ginger
2 preserved Chinese plums
(optional)
4 tablespoons oil

METHOD

1 Heat oil, fry ginger slices and garlic.
  Add water, duck, preserved plums
  and lemon, salted vegetables and
  tomatoes.
2 Boil for 1 hour until duck is tender,
  add Ve-Tsin and pepper to taste.
  More water may be added if
  necessary.

DUCK SOUP WITH SALTED VEGETABLES

FIVE KINDS OF BRAISED VEGETABLES

INGREDIENTS

100 g snow peas
10 dried mushrooms, soaked
200 g canned button mushrooms
200 g cauliflower, cut into florets
100 g canned young sweet corn
2 tablespoons cooking oil
Pinch of salt

A ½ teaspoon sugar
    ½ teaspoon salt
    Pinch of Ve-Tsin
    ½ cup water
B 2 tablespoons water
    1 tablespoon cornflour

METHOD

1 Boil the dried mushrooms, button mushrooms, cauliflower and young sweet corn in water and a little oil and salt.

2 Heat the cooking oil and fry the snow peas for 2 minutes, then add the drained boiled vegetables and **A.**

3 When liquid in pan begins to boil, add **B** and let it thicken slightly. Remove and serve.

CHICKEN RICE

INGREDIENTS

1 chicken about 1½ kg
1 cucumber, peeled and sliced
2 tomatoes, sliced
3 stalks Chinese parsley
500 g rice
2 teaspoons salt
3 tablespoons cooking oil
6 cloves garlic
1 tablespoon sesame oil

METHOD

1 Boil enough water to cover the whole chicken. Put in the chicken and bring to the boil.
2 Cover the container and reduce the temperature to simmer for 15 minutes.
3 Remove the chicken and allow it to cool. Cut into serving pieces and arrange on a serving dish. Spoon some chicken stock and the tablespoon of sesame oil over the chicken pieces. Garnish with the cucumbers, tomatoes and Chinese parsley. Put to one side.
4 Wash the rice and place in a rice cooker. Add the salt, cooking oil, garlic and measure 3 cups of stock to cook the rice. Cook for 15-20 minutes until rice is fluffy.
5 Serve the hot rice with the chicken.

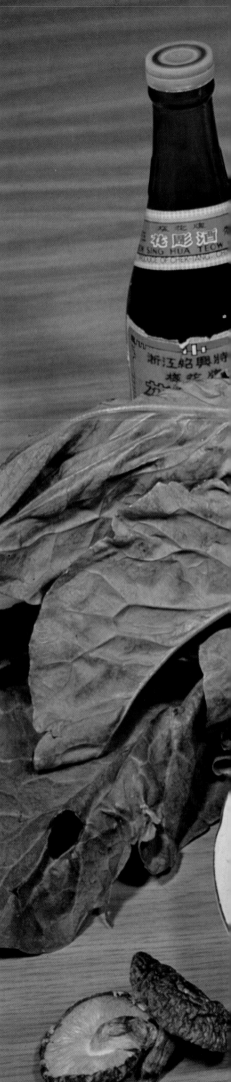

FRIED LONG BEANS

INGREDIENTS

400 g long beans, cut into 10 cm lengths
3 cups cooking oil
½ teaspoon salt

A 150 g minced pork
25 g minced preserved vegetables
2 teaspoons chopped spring onions
1 teaspoon chopped ginger

B 3 tablespoons water
1 tablespoon soy sauce
½ teaspoon sugar

METHOD

1 Heat the 3 cups of cooking oil and fry the long beans for a few minutes. Transfer the beans to a plate and mix in ½ teaspoon salt.
2 Heat 3 tablespoons of the cooking oil and fry **A** until the minced pork is cooked, then add **B**.
3 Add the long beans, cook for a few minutes and serve hot.

FRIED MUSTARD GREENS AND MUSHROOMS

INGREDIENTS

4 mustard greens
8 dried mushrooms, soaked
2 slices ginger
Pinch of Ve-Tsin
Pinch of salt
2 tablespoons oil

A 2 tablespoons oyster sauce
½ tablespoon cooking oil
1 teaspoon sugar
4 tablespoons water

METHOD

1 Remove the old leaves and harsh skin then cut the mustard greens into 2 cm pieces.
2 Heat the cooking oil and fry the ginger slices and mushrooms. Add the mustard greens and continue stir-frying.
3 Add **A**, salt and Ve-Tsin to taste. Fry for another 2 to 3 minutes and serve.

MINCED PORK IN BAMBOO CUPS

INGREDIENTS

400 g minced pork
4 dried mushrooms, soaked and
finely chopped
1 tablespoon minced spring onions
1 egg white
1 teaspoon salt
½ teaspoon Ve-Tsin
Pinch of pepper
1 tablespoon cooking wine
2 tablespoons cornflour
1 tablespoon cooking oil
10 tablespoons water

METHOD

1 Mix all ingredients and beat by
hand for ½ hour.
2 Divide mixture into 6 equal portions
and place in individual bamboo
cups. Steam for 15 minutes. Serve
hot.

*Porcelain or heatproof bowls may
be used instead of bamboo cups.*

CLAY - POT BEAN CURD

INGREDIENTS

5 pieces bean curd
100 g canned young sweet corn
100 g snow peas
100 g roast pork, sliced
2 slices ginger
1 egg, beaten
3 cups cooking oil

A 1 teaspoon salt
½ teaspoon Ve-Tsin
Pinch of pepper

B ½ tablespoon cornflour
1 tablespoon water
¾ cup hot water

METHOD

1 Slice each bean curd into two and
deep-fry in oil until golden brown.
2 Lightly stir-fry the snow peas in 2
tablespoons of oil.
3 Place bean curd, snow peas, sweet
corn, roast pork and ginger slices in
clay-pot. Add the ¾ cup of hot
water and **A** and boil for 15
minutes.
4 Add **B** and the beaten egg and
cook untii the gravy slightly
thickens. Serve hot.

33

CLAY-POT BEAN CURD

FRIED SHREDDED PORK WITH GREEN PEPPER

INGREDIENTS

200 g pork, shredded as in illustration
1 green pepper, shredded
1 stalk spring onion, shredded
1 teaspoon ginger, shredded
2 cloves garlic, chopped
5 tablespoons cooking oil
1 teaspoon salt

A ½ tablespoon cooking oil
   ½ tablespoon black soy sauce
   1 teaspoon cornflour

B 1 teaspoon soy sauce
   1 teaspoon sugar
   ½ teaspoon Ve-Tsin

METHOD

1 Season pork with **A** for 10 minutes.
2 Heat 2 tablespoons of cooking oil, and fry the shredded green chilli pepper with 1 teaspoon salt for a few minutes. Remove from pan.
3 Heat 3 tablespoons of cooking oil and fry garlic, ginger, spring onions and shredded pork for 3 minutes.
4 Add **B** and the green pepper and continue to fry until the pork is cooked. Serve hot.

FRIED SHARK'S FINS WITH EGG

INGREDIENTS

120 g prepared shark's fins
100 g crab meat
50 g canned bamboo shoots, shredded
50 g cooked ham, shredded
7 eggs
1 teaspoon salt
½ teaspoon sesame oil
½ teaspoon Ve-Tsin
3 tablespoons water
1 teaspoon soy sauce
2 tablespoons cooking oil

METHOD

1 Break all the eggs into a large bowl and combine all ingredients, except the oil. Stir thoroughly.
2 Heat some of the oil in a pan. Pour in the egg mixture and stir-fry, adding more oil during the frying, until the mixture is cooked.

FRIED RICE

INGREDIENTS

4 bowls cooked rice, about 450 g
150 g small shelled prawns
100 g lean pork, cubed
2 tablespoons green peas
4 eggs, lightly beaten
5 tablespoons cooking oil

A 1 teaspoon salt
   1 teaspoon Ve-Tsin
   ½ teaspoon pepper
   1 teaspoon sesame oil

B 1 tablespoon soy sauce
   2 tablespoons water

METHOD

1 Mix cooked rice with **A.**
2. Heat 5 tablespoons of cooking oil and fry the beaten egg, then add the rice.
3 Add the prawns, roast lean pork and green peas and stir.
4 Lastly, add **B** and continue to fry for a few minutes. Serve hot.

39

FRIED RICE

MIXED VEGETABLES DE LUXE

INGREDIENTS

20 g dried mushrooms, soaked
230 g carrots, sliced
50 g snow peas
80 g canned button mushrooms
250 g cauliflower, cut into florets
40 g canned bamboo shoots, sliced
2 tablespoons cooking oil

A ¾ cup water
½ teaspoon salt
½ teaspoon Ve-Tsin
½ teaspoon sugar
1 teaspoon soy sauce
1 teaspoon sesame oil
½ tablespoon oyster sauce
Pinch of pepper

B 1 tablespoon cornflour
1½ tablespoons water

METHOD

1 Heat the cooking oil and fry the dried mushrooms, carrots, snow peas, button mushrooms, cauliflower and bamboo shoots for a few minutes.
2 Add **A**, bring to the boil then add **B**. Serve hot.

FRIED CHICKEN WITH CASHEW NUTS

INGREDIENTS

200 g chicken breasts, diced
80 g roasted cashew nuts
5 pieces dried mushrooms,
soaked and diced
1 green pepper diced
50 g carrots, diced
1 onion, diced
2 cloves garlic, crushed
2 teaspoons light soy sauce
1 teaspoon cornflour
1 teaspoon salt
Pinch of pepper
2 slices ginger
2 tablespoons cooking oil

METHOD

1 Marinate the chicken with the
cornflour and light soy sauce for
10 minutes.
2 Heat the cooking oil and fry the
garlic, ginger and diced
mushrooms.
3 Add the chicken, green pepper,
carrot and onion and fry for a few
minutes. Add the salt and pepper
to taste.
4 Remove from heat and add the
roasted cashew nuts. Serve.

ASSORTED COLD DISH

INGREDIENTS

100 g cooked ham, sliced
100 g fried egg
200 g cooked chicken meat, sliced
100 g canned asparagus
100 g canned button mushrooms
150 g roast pork, sliced

METHOD

Arrange the well-prepared food
tastefully on a large plate and serve.

BEAN CURD WITH SPICY SAUCE

INGREDIENTS

2 cakes bean curd
120 g minced pork
1 tablespoon minced spring onion
1 slice ginger ⎤
2 red chillies ⎬ chopped
1 clove garlic ⎦
½ tablespoon bean paste
2 tablespoons black soy sauce
1 teaspoon sugar
Pinch of Ve-Tsin
¾ cup water or stock
3 tablespoons cooking oil
A 1 teaspoon cornflour
1 tablespoon water

METHOD

1 Heat the oil and fry chopped garlic,
ginger, chillies, bean paste and
minced pork for a few minutes.
2 Add black soy sauce, Ve-Tsin,
sugar and bean curd. Bring to the
boil, then add ¾ cup water or stock
and thicken with **A.**
3 Serve hot.

EGG DROP SOUP

INGREDIENTS

8 cups stock or water
300 g spinach, washed and cut
into 5 cm lengths
2 eggs, lightly beaten
8 cloud ears, soaked
1 tablespoon cooking oil
Pinch of salt
½ teaspoon soy sauce
Pinch of pepper
Pinch of Ve-Tsin

METHOD

1. Bring stock or water to the boil.
Add the cooking oil, spinach and
pre-soaked cloud ears.
2 Bring to the boil again and add
seasoning. Drop in the beaten
eggs and add pepper before
serving.

49

FRIED BEEF IN OYSTER SAUCE

INGREDIENTS

300 g beef fillet, sliced
100 g canned straw mushrooms
100 g snow peas
5 stalks of spring onions, cut into
6 cm lengths
400 g carrots, sliced
1 onion, sliced
½ tablespoon cooking wine
5 tablespoons cooking oil

Marinade for Beef

A 1 teaspoon bicarbonate of soda
   ½ teaspoon Ve-Tsin
   ½ teaspoon sugar
   1 teaspoon black soy sauce
   ½ teaspoon sesame oil
   2 tablespoons water
   1 tablespoon cornflour
   ½ tablespoon cooking oil

Gravy

B 5 tablespoons water
   ½ teaspoon salt
   ½ teaspoon Ve-Tsin
   2 tablespoons oyster sauce
   ½ teaspoon sesame oil
   Pinch of pepper
   ½ tablespoon cornflour

METHOD

1. Season beef with **A** for 10 minutes.
2. Heat 3 tablespoons cooking oil and fry beef for ½ minute and remove from heat.
3. Heat 2 tablespoons cooking oil and fry ginger slices, straw mushrooms, snow peas, carrots, spring onions and onion slices. Add ½ tablespoon cooking wine.
4. Add **B** and fry until all ingredients are cooked.
5. Serve hot.

FRIED BEEF IN OYSTER SAUCE

STEAMED FISH

INGREDIENTS

1 Pomfret about 500 g
2 dried mushrooms, soaked and sliced
5 stalks spring onions, 2 cut into 4 cm lengths
1 stalk of Chinese parsley
1 red chilli, shredded
1 teaspoon ginger, shredded
1 tomato, sliced
1 teaspoon soy sauce
1 tablespoon cooking oil
Pinch of Ve-Tsin

A 2 teaspoons salt
½ teaspoon Ve-Tsin
½ teaspoon sugar
Pinch of pepper

METHOD

1 Remove entrails from the pomfret and clean it. Make three cuts on each side of the pomfret and season with **A** for 10 minutes.

2 Transfer the seasoned pomfret to a dish with three spring onions placed at the bottom.

3 Garnish with shredded chilli, spring onions and tomato slices. Then add Ve-Tsin, soy sauce and 1 tablespoon of cooking oil and steam for 12-14 minutes. Serve immediately.

Pomfret may be substituted by other white fish.

SAUTÉD BEAN CURD

INGREDIENTS

2 cakes bean curd, sliced
2 dried mushrooms, soaked and shredded
50 g bamboo shoots, sliced
50 g snow peas
1 stalk spring onion
3 red chillies, shredded
2 slices ginger
1 tablespoon chilli bean paste
200 g lean pork, sliced
3 tablespoons cooking oil

A 1 tablespoon soy sauce
   1 teaspoon sugar
   1 tablespoon cooking wine
   1 teaspoon sesame oil

B ½ tablespoon cornflour
   1 tablespoon water

METHOD

1 Fry the bean curd slices in the heated cooking oil until golden brown.
2 Fry the ginger slices, then add the mushrooms, snow peas, lean pork and bamboo shoots. Fry for a further few minutes.
3 Add the chilli bean paste, spring onions and shredded chillies and continue frying.
4 Lastly, add well-stirred **A** and **B** and cook until the gravy thickens. Serve immediately.

DEEP FRIED PRAWNS

INGREDIENTS

12 large prawns, unshelled
1½ tablespoons ginger, chopped
5 cloves garlic, chopped
2 red chillies, chopped
5 tablespoons cooking oil

A 1 teaspoon salt
   1 teaspoon sugar
   3 tablespoons water

METHOD

1 Heat the cooking oil and fry ginger, garlic and chillies.
2 Add the prawns and fry until they turn red, then add **A.** Simmer until the gravy thickens. Remove and serve.

55

DEEP FRIED PRAWNS

ROAST CHICKEN

INGREDIENTS
1 clean chicken about 1 kg
5 small onions
4 cloves garlic
2 tablespoons black soy sauce
1 tablespoon cooking oil
½ teaspoon pepper

METHOD
1 Pound onions and garlic using a mortar and pestle* and mix with pepper and black soy sauce.
2 Spread the pounded mixture over the outside of the chicken. Pour the tablespoon of cooking oil over it.
3 Stuff the inside of the chicken with the remaining mixture.
4 Place the chicken in an oven and roast for 45 minutes at 190°C.

* A food processor may be used to grind the onions and garlic.

DEEP SAUCED BEAN CURD

INGREDIENTS
10 pieces of bean curd, each cut into 2 diagonally
¼ cup water mixed with ½ teaspoon salt
2 tablespoons cooking oil
3 cups cooking oil

A 100 g minced pork
   50 g fish meat
   20 g salted fish
   4 dried mushrooms, soaked and chopped
   1 tablespoon salt
   1 teaspoon salt
   ½ teaspoon pepper
   ½ tablespoon cooking wine
   5 tablespoons water

B 1 tablespoon black soy sauce
   1 teaspoon sesame oil
   2 tablespoons oyster sauce
   ½ teaspoon Ve-Tsin

C 1 tablespoon cornflour
   2 tablespoons water

METHOD
1 Beat mixture **A** by hand for ½ hour.
2 Make slits in the halved bean curd and stuff with the beaten mixture **A** and seal the openings with salt water.
3 Heat the 3 cups of cooking oil and deep-fry the prepared bean curd until golden brown. Remove and drain.
4 Heat 2 tablespoons of cooking oil. Add **B** and bring to the boil. Add **C** and the drained bean curd. Mix well and serve immediately.

MUSHROOM BACON SOUP

INGREDIENTS

15 dried mushrooms, soaked
2 slices bacon, cut into small pieces
100 g chicken breast, cubed
5 cups water

A 1 teaspoon salt
1 teaspoon cooking wine
Pinch of pepper and Ve-Tsin

METHOD

1 Boil 5 cups of water.
2 Add mushrooms and boil for 5 minutes.
3 Add chicken meat and bacon slices.
4 Lastly, add **A** and continue to boil for a few more minutes before serving.

SWEET AND SOUR FISH

INGREDIENTS

400 g fish meat, sliced
5 tablespoons cornflour
1 cup oil

A 1 teaspoon salt
1 teaspoon pepper

B 3 tablespoons sugar
2 tablespoons vinegar
1 teaspoon salt
½ cup water
3 tablespoons tomato sauce

C 1 tablespoon cornflour
2 tablespoons water

METHOD

1 Season fish meat with **A** for 10 minutes. Coat the fish with cornflour and deep-fry in oil until golden brown. Drain.
2 Heat 1 tablespoon of oil, add **B** and bring to the boil before adding **C**. When the gravy thickens, pour over the deep fried fish. Serve immediately.

CHINESE CABBAGE WITH HAM

INGREDIENTS

600 g Chinese cabbage, cut into small pieces
200 g cooked ham
2 slices ginger
3 tablespoons cooking oil

A 1 teaspoon salt
    1 teaspoon sugar
    ½ teaspoon Ve-Tsin

B ½ teaspoon cornflour
    1½ tablespoons water

METHOD

1 Heat the cooking oil and fry the slices of ginger.
2 Add the Chinese cabbage and fry until soft, adding **A** and covering the pan. Allow to simmer for a few minutes and add **B.**
3 Add the cooked ham to the cabbage, heat for another few minutes and serve.

SWEET AND SOUR PORK

INGREDIENTS

300 g pork tenderloin, cubed 3 cm
1 onion
1 green pepper   } cubed 2 cm
1 red chilli
½ cucumber
2 cups cooking oil for deep-frying

A 1 tablespoon soy sauce
    ½ tablespoon cooking oil
    4 tablespoons cornflour
    2 tablespoons tomato sauce

B 1 tablespoon vinegar
    2 tablespoons sugar
    1 teaspoon salt
    ¾ cup water

C 1 tablespoon cornflour
    2 tablespoons water

METHOD

1 Season pork with **A** for 15 minutes. Coat pork with cornflour and fry in oil until a golden colour.
2 Heat oil and fry onions, green pepper, chilli and cucumber. Add **B** and bring to the boil.
3 Thicken with **C,** add fried pork and mix well. Serve hot.

SWEET AND SOUR PORK

DRUNKEN CHICKEN

INGREDIENTS

1 chicken about 1½ kg
½ cup Chinese wine
½ cup brandy
1 lettuce leaf
1 stalk Chinese parsley
2 tomatoes, sliced
1 teaspoon salt

METHOD

1. Boil the chicken in enough water to cover. When tender remove from heat and soak in cold water until cold.
2 Cut the chicken into pieces and place in a large bowl with the skin-side downwards.
3 Pour the Chinese wine and brandy over the chicken and let it soak for 5 to 6 hours.
4 To serve, pour the wine into a bowl, arrange the chicken on a serving plate and pour the wine over the chicken again.
5 Garnish with lettuce, tomatoes and Chinese parsley.

FRIED PORK WITH PRESERVED VEGETABLES

INGREDIENTS

200 g pork
100 g canned preserved vegetables, shredded
8 dried mushrooms, soaked and shredded
1 clove garlic, chopped
1 stalk spring onion, shredded
3 tablespoons cooking oil

A 1 teaspoon soy sauce
   1 teaspoon cornflour
   ½ teaspoon sesame oil

B 3 tablespoons water
   ½ teaspoon Ve-Tsin

C ½ teaspoon cornflour
   1 tablespoon water

METHOD

1 Season the shredded pork with **A** for 15 minutes.
2 Heat the cooking oil and fry the garlic and mushrooms. Then add the pork and preserved vegetables and fry together.
3 Add **B** and fry for a few minutes and add **C** and shredded onions. Cook for a further few minutes. Serve.

STEAMED - POT STEWED CHICKEN

INGREDIENTS

1 tender chicken, cleaned and cut into pieces
1 slice ginger
½ teaspoon salt
6 pieces dried mushrooms, soaked
2 teaspoons cooking wine (optional)

METHOD

1 Place all ingredients into a heat-proof bowl or a Chinese steam-pot. Add ⅓ cup of water.
2 Place the bowl with the ingredients on a stand in a larger stewing pot containing water.
3 Steam for two hours until the chicken is thoroughly cooked and ready to serve.

See notes on "Steaming", page 95.

STEAMED-POT STEWED CHICKEN

FRIED SPINACH WITH ABALONE

INGREDIENTS

1 canned abalone, cut into slices
4 stalks spinach, cleaned and cut
into 6 cm lengths
1 teaspoon oyster sauce
1 teaspoon sesame oil
1 teaspoon salt
Pinch of Ve-Tsin and pepper
3 tablespoons cooking oil
A ½ tablespoon cornflour
1 tablespoon water

METHOD

1 Heat the cooking oil and fry
spinach for a few minutes. Add
the oyster sauce, sesame oil, salt
and pepper.
2 Add the abalone slices and fry for
a few minutes then add **A** and
bring to the boil. Serve hot.

STEWED BEEF IN CLAY-POT

INGREDIENTS

500 g topside steak, cut into small pieces
2 slices ginger
1 star anise
small piece of dried Chinese orange peel
2 cloves garlic
1 cup water
2 tablespoons cooking oil

A ½ teaspoon salt
    ½ teaspoon Ve-Tsin
    1 tablespoon black soy sauce
    ½ tablespoon cooking oil
    Pinch of pepper
    1 teaspoon sugar

METHOD

1 Season beef with **A** for 10 minutes.
2 Heat cooking oil in a clay-pot. Fry the garlic then add the beef and fry for a further few minutes.
3 Add 1 cup of water, star anise, orange peel and ginger slices.
4 Reduce temperature and simmer for 6 hours.

MEAT SAUCE NOODLES

INGREDIENTS

1 kg noodles
200 g prepared bean paste (see below)
2 tablespoons cooking wine
400 g minced pork
2 tablespoons chopped onions
2 tablespoons cooking oil
1 cucumber, shredded

METHOD

1 Heat 2 tablespoons of cooking oil and fry the minced pork until cooked. Add the chopped onion and prepared bean paste. Add the cooking wine and continue frying for 5 minutes.

2 Boil the noodles and serve with the meat sauce and shredded cucumber.

METHOD OF PREPARING BEAN PASTE

½ cup bean paste
3 tablespoons sugar
½ teaspoon Ve-Tsin
4 tablespoons flour
½ cup water
4 tablespoons cooking oil

Heat 4 tablespoons of cooking oil. Fry flour till brown, add bean paste, sugar, Ve-Tsin and water. Fry thoroughly.

MILKY CHICKEN

INGREDIENTS

1 chicken about 1½ kg
8 dried mushrooms, soaked and sliced
1 small carrot, sliced
2 tablespoons cooking oil

A 3 tablespoons evaporated milk
   1 rice bowl of stock
   ½ teaspoon Ve-Tsin
   ½ teaspoon sugar
   1 teaspoon sesame oil
   Pinch of pepper

B 1½ tablespoons cornflour
   1 tablespoon water

C 1 egg white
   1 tablespoon water

METHOD

1 Boil chicken in enough water until tender. Remove and cut into pieces. Pour **A** over chicken pieces and leave for 15 minutes. Drain off the liquid into a bowl and put aside.

2 Boil carrot slices and dried mushrooms in water until cooked. Remove and drain.

3 Heat 2 tablespoons of cooking oil, add **A** and bring to the boil. Add **B** and stir until mixture thickens.

4 Add **C**, carrots, mushrooms and chicken pieces and bring to the boil again.

STEAMED CHICKEN WITH BIRD'S NEST

INGREDIENTS

1 chicken about 1 kg, remove
bones and cut into pieces
40 g clean bird's nest
3 cups water
1 slice ginger
2 teaspoons salt
½ teaspoon Ve-Tsin

METHOD

Place all ingredients in a bowl and
steam for 2 hours. Serve.

FISH IN DUAL STYLES

Directions for preparation of fish

1　Take one yellow croaker about
　500 g. Remove the scales, gills,
　entrails and clean it.
2　Remove the head and fillet the
　meat, discarding the bones. Also
　cut the head into two, lengthways.
3　Season the fish with a teaspoon of
　salt and a little Ve-Tsin and leave
　for 10 minutes.
4　Coat the fish with cornflour and
　deep-fry in oil.

SWEET AND SOUR FISH

INGREDIENTS

1 side of fish with head
2 tablespoons cooking oil

A　5 tablespoons water
　2 tablespoons tomato sauce
　½ tablespoon chilli sauce
　2 tablespoons sugar
　1 teaspoon salt
　1 tablespoon vinegar
　¼ teaspoon Ve-Tsin

B　½ tablespoon cornflour
　1 tablespoon water

METHOD

1　Heat the cooking oil, add **A** and
　bring to the boil.
2　Add **B** to thicken gravy. Pour over
　fish and serve.

BLACK SOY SAUCE FISH

INGREDIENTS

1 side of fish with head
4 cloves garlic, chopped
½ teaspoon Ve-Tsin
½ tablespoon ginger, shredded
2 tablespoons black soy sauce
2 tablespoons cooking oil

METHOD

1　Heat 2 tablespoons oil and fry the
　garlic and ginger. Add the soy
　sauce and Ve-Tsin.
2　Coat the fish on both sides with
　sauce and serve.

*Croaker may be substituted by
other similar varieties of fish.*

JELLIED CHICKEN AND HAM

INGREDIENTS

½ chicken
200 g cooked ham

A ½ tablespoon cooking wine
   3 tablespoons hot water
   ½ teaspoon salt
   ½ tablespoon gelatine
   ½ teaspoon Ve-Tsin

METHOD

1 Boil the chicken in water with a pinch of salt.

2 Remove the bones from the chicken and cut the meat into uniform slices. Do the same with the cooked ham.

3 Arrange the chicken and ham slices in alternate layers in a bowl. Add **A** and steam for 5 minutes. When cool, place the bowl in the refrigerator to set.

4 To serve, turn out on to a serving dish and garnish.

BEAN PASTE PASTRY

INGREDIENTS
300 g red bean paste
100 g flour
2 eggs
10 tablespoons water

METHOD
1 Put flour in a bowl and add the water and eggs. Mix thoroughly and filter the mixture.
2 Rub a frying pan evenly with oil, heat and pour half of batter into the pan. When pancake is cooked remove from heat.
3 Repeat with the rest of batter.
4 Spread the bean paste on the pancakes and fold into rectangles.
5 Fry again in the frying pan with a little oil until fairly brown and crisp. Slice and serve.

SWEET RED BEAN SOUP

INGREDIENTS
2 cups red beans
Small piece of dried Chinese orange peel
400 g rock sugar
200 g lotus seeds, prepared as on page 95
6 cups water

METHOD
1 Wash the red beans and place into a saucepan. Add lotus seeds, orange peel and 6 cups of water. Bring to the boil and continue simmering until beans are half cooked.
2 Add the rock sugar and continue to simmer until the beans are well cooked. Serve hot.

87

SWEET RED BEAN SOUP

SPRING ROLLS

INGREDIENTS

150 g pork, shredded
100 g bean sprouts, cleaned
100 g carrots, shredded
3 stalks spring onions, shredded
5 pieces dried mushrooms,
soaked and shredded
10 pieces spring roll wrappers

A ½ teaspoon Ve-Tsin
   2 teaspoons salt
   1 teaspoon sugar
   2 teaspoons oyster sauce
   1 teaspoon sesame oil

B 1 tablespoon cornflour
   2 tablespoons water

C 2 tablespoons plain flour
   1 tablespoon water
   3 tablespoons cooking oil

METHOD

1 Heat 3 tablespoons cooking oil
and fry mushrooms, pork, bean
sprouts and carrots for a few
minutes and add **A**. Fry for
another few minutes and add **B**.

2 Divide the mixture into 10 equal
portions. Put each portion on a
spring roll wrapper and form into a
roll. Seal the ends with **C**.

3 Fry the spring rolls in a suitable
amount of oil until brown and
crispy. Serve hot.

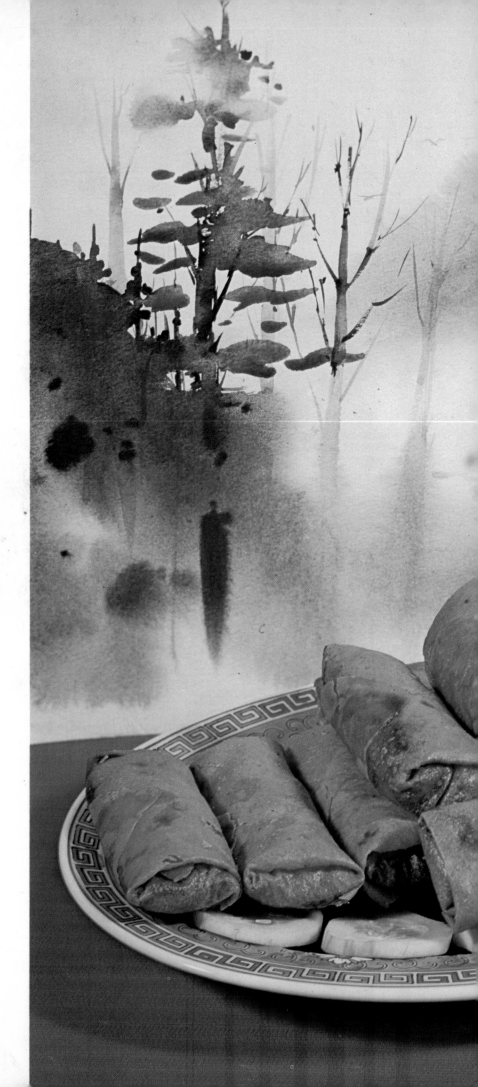

ALMOND JELLY

INGREDIENTS

1 packet Agar Agar powder
400 g can evaporated milk
1 cup sugar
1 tablespoon almond essence
4 cups water

METHOD

1 Place water, sugar and Agar Agar powder in a saucepan. Boil to dissolve the sugar and Agar Agar. Stir evenly during boiling.
2 Add the evaporated milk and the almond essence, and stir thoroughly.
3 Pour the Agar Agar mixture into a mould and place in a refrigerator to set.
4 Remove from mould to serve. Decorate with fresh or canned fruit.

SWEET WHITE CLOUD EARS SOUP

INGREDIENTS

25 g white cloud ears, soaked for
2 hours
200 g rock sugar
4 cups water
10 water chestnuts, skinned and
sliced

METHOD

1 Place white cloud ears with the
water in a heat-proof bowl.
2 Steam for 2 hours, then add rock
sugar and water chestnuts.
Continue to steam until rock sugar
is dissolved. Serve hot.

SEASONING AND SPICES

Abalone are a salt water shellfish. The canned variety is usually used in Chinese cooking.

Agar Agar is the base for jellies. Substitute with gelatine.

Bamboo Shoots are a crisp root vegetable. It is available canned and is usually sliced to cook with other vegetables.

Bean Curd is a firm custard-like cake from soy bean milk. It has a smooth elastic-like texture and a bland taste. It is a very high protein food and is used as a meat substitute in Chinese cooking.

Bird's Nests are transparent, gelatinous strands coating nests of swiftlets found in S.E.Asia. Soak in water for an hour before use.

Chinese Parsley also known as coriander is used fresh as a garnish.

Cinnamon is a bark-like spice with a strong flavour used in all types of cooking. It may be obtained whole or ground; usually removed before serving if used whole.

Cloud Ears are irregular-shaped, edible fungi. They are spongy textured. Available in two varieties: black and white. Soak before use.

Cooking Wine used in Chinese cooking is usually a rice wine. It may be substituted with ordinary cooking wine or sherry.

Dried Chinese Orange Peel is the dried skin of Chinese oranges or tangerines. Used sparingly in flavouring.

Dried Mushrooms referred to in this book are the black Chinese variety. They have to be soaked in water for ½ hour before use. The stems are always removed.

Dried Scallops are shellfish with a delicate flavour. Used in soups and vegetables dished.

Ginger is the root of the ginger plant. Used for flavouring of meat and vegetables.

Lotus Beans Seeds are small, delicately flavoured seeds of the water-lily. Usually available dried. Soak for 10 minutes, halve and remove green bitter shoot before use.

Oyster Sauce is skimmed from fermented oysters preserved in brine. Used for seasoning meat and vegetable dishes.

Preserved Chinese Plums are pickled plums used in fish cookery.

Preserved Lemon is a dried and sweetened lemon used in flavouring of foods.

Preserved Vegetables are vegetable stems pickled in brine and hot pepper. Available in cans.

Red Bean Paste is a thick sweet paste of red beans. Made from steamed red bean and sugar. Also available in cans.

Red Dates are a dried fruit used in soups. Soak in warm water before use.

Rock Sugar is sugar in crystallized form. It is available in any Chinese provision store.

Sesame Oil is a potent, fragrant oil of the sesame seed. Use sparingly.

Shark's Fins are the dried cartilage from the fins of sharks. They are soaked in hot water for an hour to soften before cooking.

Soy Bean Paste is a thick salty paste made from black or yellow soy bean. Used in seasoning of meat or vegetable dishes.

Soy Sauce is a sauce made from fermented soy beans. It is very salty and is found in two varieties: black or light brown. The light brown variety is generally used. Black is used where specified. Use sparingly.

Spring Roll Wrappers are thin squares of pastry used for spring rolls. They are made from flour, egg and water. Available from the freezer section of any Chinese supermarket.

Star-Anise is a star-shaped spice used either crushed or whole to flavour meat or poultry.

Ve-Tsin is a derivation of monosodium glutamate and is used to enhance the natural flavour of foods. The equivalent in America and Europe is "Accent". Use very sparingly.

Water-Chestnuts are nut-sized bulbs with tough brown skins and crisp white meat. Usually obtained in cans already prepared for use.

METHODS OF CHINESE COOKING

Cold Mixing is usually the method used for the appetizer. It consists of one or more ingredients served cold. It is referred to as the "cold" or "combination" dish.

Deep-Frying. A large amount of oil is heated in a deep pan or Chinese wok until smoking hot. Ingredients, which are usually batter-coated, are plunged in a few at a time and left to cook until golden brown. Deep fried foods are to be drained as they are removed from the oil.

Stir-Frying. A small amount of oil is heated in a pan or wok, until smoking hot. Ingredients are quickly added and stirred to cook for 2 - 3 minutes and served. Usually the method is used for vegetables and canned sliced meat or seafood.

Roasting is done by first marinating meats and placing them into an oven or on an open grill to cook.

Steaming. A steamer or large pot with a fitted cover is filled with sufficient water and is brought to the boil. The heat proof dish holding the food to be steamed is then placed on a small stand and the fitted cover put in position. To improvise, an overturned heat-proof soup plate may be used as a stand.

In steaming, the intensity of heat depends on the type of food being cooked. Foods such as meat, fish, dumplings, etc., should be steamed at a high temperature. Eggs, pork buns, etc., should be steamed at a low temperature. For longer steaming times, the level of simmering water has to be maintained by topping up with hot water occasionally.

Stewing requires the ingredients to be browned first and then placed in a stewing pot with plenty of water and cooked for a period of time at a low heat producing a thick gravy.

Note. All recipes serve 2 - 4 persons as a main dish. As part of a 6-course Chinese meal, each recipe will serve 8 - 10 persons.

WEIGHTS AND MEASURES

In the Imperial and American Systems, measures in weight are similar. Measures in volume are different, and the following tables show the equivalents:

SPOON MEASURES:

Imperial	American
1 teaspoon (5 ml) (tsp)	1 ¼ teaspoons
1 tablespoon (20 ml) (tbsp)	1 ¼ tablespoons

LIQUID MEASURES:

Imperial	American	
20 fluid oz	16 fluid oz	1 pint
10 fluid oz	8 fluid oz	1 cup

WEIGHT:

Imperial	Metric	Working equivalent
1 oz	28.35 g	32 g
2 oz	56.70 g	63 g
4 oz	113.40 g	125 g
8 oz	226.80 g	250 g
1.0 lb	453.00 g	500 g
1.1 lb	½ kilo	
2.2 lb	1 kilo	

LIQUID MEASURES:

Imperial	Exact conversion	Working equivalent
¼ pint (1 gill)	142 ml	150 ml
½ pint	284 ml	300 ml
1 pint	568 ml	600 ml
1 ¾ pints	994 ml	1 litre

LINEAR MEASURES:

English	Metric
1 in	2 ½ cm
2 in	5 cm
3 in	7 ½ cm
6 in	15 cm

It is useful to note for easy reference that:
1 kilogramme (1000 grammes) = 2.2 lb therefore
½ kilo (500 grammes) roughly = 1 lb
1 litre roughly = 1¾ Imperial pints therefore
½ litre roughly = 1 Imperial pint

OVEN TEMPERATURES:

The following chart gives the conversions from degrees Fahrenheit to degrees Centigrade:

°F	°C	
225	110	very cool or very slow
250	130	
275	140	cool or slow
300	150	
325	170	very moderate
350	180	moderate
375	190	moderately hot
400	200	
425	220	hot
450	230	very hot
475	240	

INDEX